✳ Smithsonian
A REVOLUTIONARY WAR

TIMELINE

BY ELIZABETH RAUM

CAPSTONE PRESS
a capstone imprint

Capstone Press
1710 Roe Crest Drive
North Mankato, Minnesota 56003
www.capstonepub.com

The name of the Smithsonian Institution and the sunburst logo
are registered trademarks of the Smithsonian Institution.
For more information, please visit www.si.edu.

Our very special thanks to F. Robert van der Linden, chairman of the Aeronautics
Division at the National Air and Space Museum, Smithsonian Institution, for his
curatorial review. Capstone would also like to thank Kealy Wilson, Smithsonian
Institution Product Development Manager, and the following at Smithsonian
Enterprises: Ellen Nanney, Licensing Manager; Brigid Ferraro, Vice President,
Education and Consumer Products; Carol LeBlanc, Senior Vice President,
Education and Consumer Products.

Library of Congress Cataloging-in-Publication Data
Raum, Elizabeth.
 A Revolutionary War timeline / by Elizabeth Raum.
pages cm. — (Smithsonian war timelines)
Includes index.
Summary: "An illustrated timeline of the Revolutionary War"— Provided by
publisher.
 ISBN 978-1-4765-4157-0 (library binding)
 ISBN 978-1-4765-5177-7 (paperback)
1. United States—History—Revolution, 1775–1783—Chronology—Juvenile
literature. I. Title.
E209.R27 2014
973.3—dc23   2013032305

Editorial Credits
Kristen Mohn, editor; Ted Williams, designer; Svetlana Zhurkin, media researcher;
Kathy McColley, production specialist

Printed in the United States of America in Brainerd, Minnesota.
092013   007774BANGS14

TABLE OF CONTENTS

THE
REVOLUTIONARY WAR

A successful revolution is a new beginning. The revolution of the British colonists in North America was the beginning of a new nation—the United States of America. Born of battles and bloodshed, the young country grew to lead the world.

Before the dramatic events of the late 1700s that spurred the revolution, Great Britain controlled the American colonies. British kings appointed governors to act on their behalf in each of the 13 colonies. They enforced British laws, halted rebellions, and reported directly to the king. Each colony had its own legislature, but the British governor, the British king, and the British Parliament were really in charge.

The colonies had acted independently of one another. But concerns over increased British taxes and unfair rulings brought them together. "No taxation without representation" became a rallying cry. At the time Great Britain was fighting two costly wars. The French and Indian War (1754–1763) took place in North America and the Seven Years War (1756–1763) in Europe. The British Parliament increased taxes on its colonies to help pay for the costs of war.

Most American colonists thought of themselves as British. Many had family in England, traded with England, and followed English styles and customs. But the new taxes tested their loyalty. Rebellious colonists called themselves patriots. Those who remained loyal to England called themselves loyalists.

The Continental Congress hoped to find peaceful solutions to the problems with Great Britain. That proved impossible. In 1776 Congress declared the American colonies independent. The war was on! Colonies began overthrowing their British governors and appointing their own leaders. George Washington, leader of the Continental Army, rallied his troops and braced for battle. So did the British.

It would not be an easy war. The colonies had to build, train, and supply an army. The British had well-trained and well-equipped solders, but they had to wage a war far from home. Communication across the Atlantic could take weeks or months, and commanders were forced to make decisions without guidance. Even within the colonies, communication was difficult.

This book presents a timeline of the most important events of the Revolution, from the colonists' first desires for freedom to their ultimate victory. The dramatic action of the war tells the incredible story of a hard-won independence.

GROWING UNREST

British Parliament passes the Sugar Act and the Currency Act to raise money from colonists to help pay debts from the French and Indian War.

The Stamp Act taxes all printed materials. The Quartering Act requires colonists to house British troops.

The Townshend Acts tax imported glass, lead, paints, paper, and tea. Colonists boycott these goods.

March 5

After Boston colonists harass a British soldier, British troops fire on the crowd, killing five colonists and wounding six. It becomes known as the Boston Massacre. Outrage over the killings helps to unite the colonists.

 **1764** 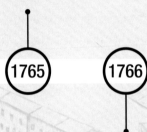 **1765** **1766** **1767** **1770**

Massachusetts forms the Committee of Correspondence. Similar committees are formed in other colonies. They encourage cooperation, aid, and communication throughout the colonies.

Months of protest convince Parliament to repeal the Stamp Act.

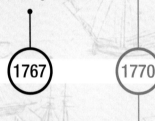

COLONY	POPULATION	COLONY	POPULATION
Virginia (Va.)	447,000	South Carolina (S.C.)	124,200
Massachusetts (Mass.)	266,600	New Jersey (N.J.)	117,400
Pennsylvania (Pa.)	240,100	New Hampshire (N.H.)	62,400
Maryland (Md.)	202,600	Rhode Island (R.I.)	58,200
North Carolina (N.C.)	197,200	Delaware (Del.)	35,500
Connecticut (Conn.)	183,900	Georgia (Ga.)	23,400
New York (N.Y.)	162,900	||||||||||||||	||||||||||||||

Population of the 13 American colonies reaches more than 2 million.

original 13 colonies

March–June

British Parliament passes the Intolerable Acts to punish colonies for rebelling. The acts close the port of Boston, limit the rights of the Massachusetts Colony, install a military government under British General—and now Governor—Thomas Gage, and forbid town meetings without British approval.

Sept. 5–Oct. 26

The First Continental Congress meets in Philadelphia. Twelve colonies send 56 delegates, including John Adams and Samuel Adams (Mass.), George Washington and Patrick Henry (Va.), Philip Livingston (N.Y.), John and Edward Rutledge (S.C.), and many others who will become leaders in the fight for independence. They ask King George III to change his policies. They organize boycotts of British goods.

1773

1774

Dec. 16

Colonists dressed as American Indians raid ships in Boston Harbor and dump tea overboard to protest the tax on tea. This becomes known as the Boston Tea Party.

May 10

Great Britain taxes tea.

Oct. 14

Congress adopts a declaration of rights stating that colonists are entitled to "life, liberty, and property."

FIRST SHOTS OF THE REVOLUTION

April 1

New York Assembly requires all men ages 16–50 to join militias.

April 14

General Gage receives orders to suppress the rebellion by force if needed.

April 19

Minutemen and Redcoats clash at Lexington and Concord. British troops return to Boston under fire. News travels throughout the colonies. The gunfire is considered the first shot of the revolution and is often called "the shot heard around the world." Massachusetts militiamen call themselves Minutemen because they can be ready in a minute. British forces are called Redcoats because they wear red uniforms.

1775

April 18

General Gage orders 700 British soldiers to destroy weapons stored in Concord, Mass. Paul Revere and William Dawes ride to warn patriots in Concord and Lexington.

March 23

Patrick Henry declares, "Give me liberty or give me death," in a speech to colonial Virginia leaders. The colony orders each county to form a militia.

May 15

Congress tells the colonies to prepare for war by establishing militias, gathering rifles and ammunition, and stockpiling food and clothing for the soldiers.

May 19

More British troops arrive in Boston.

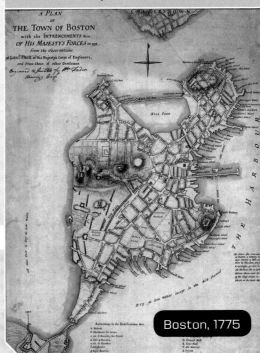

Boston, 1775

May 1

New York colonists gather weapons and begin military training.

April 21–22

New Hampshire and Rhode Island militias march to Boston.

May 30

Colonists report severe shortages of food and fuel.

April 25

Baltimore patriots seize military supplies.

May 10

American forces led by patriots Ethan Allen and Benedict Arnold capture the British Fort Ticonderoga in New York. Arnold, a general in the Continental Army, later switches sides and becomes a traitor to the Americans.

The Second Continental Congress meets in Philadelphia.

May 24

John Hancock, Massachusetts merchant and patriot, is elected president of the Second Continental Congress. Later he becomes the first to sign the Declaration of Independence.

PREPARING FOR WAR

1775

June
Colonists in Virginia, New York, and Connecticut raid British supply depots. They steal weapons and gunpowder. Such raids increase as war nears.

June 1
Continental Congress decides not to advance into or attack Canada, which is under British rule.

June 4
Ethan Allen reports that Canadians fired on a patriot scouting party.

June 8
Lord Dunmore, the British governor of Virginia, flees to a British warship at Yorktown.

June 10
John Adams, who later becomes the first vice president and second president of the United States, suggests that Congress organize an army.

June 12
Rhode Island General Assemly establishes a navy.

June 14–15
Congress establishes a Continental Army and appoints George Washington (a Virginia farmer and former commander of Virginia colonial forces) as general and commander in chief.

June 17

The Battle of Bunker Hill, actually fought at Breed's Hill, is the first major battle of the Revolution. The British win by taking control of the hill, but lose half their men in the battle.

July 5–8

Congress appeals directly to King George III with the Olive Branch Petition. Members vow loyalty to the king, saying they will not seek independence. However, they protest British trade and tax laws and ask to discuss them with Parliament. The attempt fails.

George III

July 26

Patriot Benjamin Franklin begins service as postmaster general for the first American Post Office.

June 16

Colonels Daniel Putnam and William Prescott post patriot troops on Breed's Hill near Bunker Hill in Boston.

June 27

Congress approves an invasion of Canada in hopes of bringing Canada into the war on the patriot side. Canada remains loyal to Britain.

July 13

The Continental Congress seeks to enter into a peace agreement with Indian nations that will support independence. Congress encourages Indians "to remain at home, and not join either side, but to keep the hatchet buried deep."

OPEN REBELLION

1775

July/August

King George III, lacking enough British soldiers, buys the services of soldiers called Hessians from the German state of Hesse-Cassel. Eventually soldiers come from other German provinces, and all are known as Hessians. About 30,000 Hessians fight in North America. About 5,000 stay after the war.

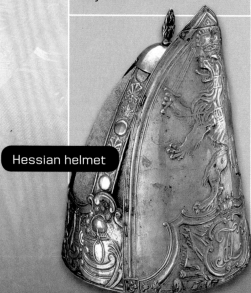

Hessian helmet

Aug. 23

King George III issues a statement declaring that colonists are in a state of open rebellion.

September

Forces under patriot Ethan Allen invade Canada to attack Montreal. The mission fails and on September 25 Allen is captured and imprisoned by the British. Meanwhile, his brother Ira Allen asks Congress to recognize Vermont's independence. Congress refuses because Vermont is considered part of New York.

Sept. 14

Colonists capture Fort Johnson, S.C.

Oct. 24–25

Colonists defend
Hampton, Va., from
British attack.

Nov. 13

American troops
capture and
occupy Montreal.

eastern Virginia, 1775

Nov. 10

Congress founds the
U.S. Marine Corps.

Dec. 9

Patriots defeat British troops at Great Bridge, Va.

November

Virginia Governor Lord Dunmore
promises freedom to all slaves who
join British forces, and 800 do so.
Some wear the emblem "Liberty to
the Slaves." Later British General
Henry Clinton promises protection to
slaves who desert the rebel forces.
Slave owners in the South and
in New York's Hudson Valley
are outraged by the offer.

Nov. 28

Congress establishes the
Navy of the United Colonies.

Dec. 14

Patriot forces occupy
Norfolk, Va.

RECLAIMING
BOSTON

Jan. 1
The Continental Army flies the Grand Union flag.

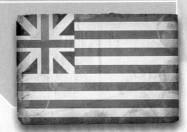

Jan. 22
South Carolina patriots agree to allow "able-bodied negro men" to help defend Charlestown, which is later renamed Charleston.

February
The British take control of Boston and take over patriot ships for military use.

Feb. 27
Patriots defeat loyalists near Wilmington, N.C.

1776

Jan. 9
Benjamin Franklin helps political activist Thomas Paine publish a pamphlet called *Common Sense*. It is an instant success and convinces many colonists that revolution against Great Britain makes sense.

COMMON SENSE;

ADDRESSED TO THE

INHABITANTS

OF

AMERICA,

On the following interesting

SUBJECTS.

I. Of the Origin and Design of Government in general, with concise Remarks on the English Constitution.
II. Of Monarchy and Hereditary Succession.
III. Thoughts on the present State of American Affairs.
IV. Of the present Ability of America, with some miscellaneous Reflections.

Man knows no Master save creating Heaven,
Or those whom choice and common good ordain.
THOMSON.

PHILADELPHIA;
Printed, and Sold, by R. BELL, in Third-Street.
MDCCLXXVI.

March
Congress fears British attacks on New York City and North and South Carolina.

WEAPONS OF WAR

Soldiers in the Continental Army provided their own weapons. Most soldiers used a flintlock musket, which had to be reloaded after each shot. Three shots per minute was the normal rate of firing. Rifles were slower to load, but they were more accurate than muskets. Many rifles and muskets had a bayonet, a knife-shaped weapon under the muzzle. Bayonets, knives, and swords were used for close fighting. The Continental Army also relied on artillery fire. Artillery included mortars, howitzers, and cannons. Mortars fired sacks of stones and scrap metal. Howitzers fired explosive shells filled with gunpowder. Cannon balls ranged in weight from 2 to 50 pounds (900 grams to 23 kilograms).

March 2

Patriot artillery bombards Boston.

March 2–5

The Navy of the United Colonies raids British naval bases on the islands of the Bahamas. It captures the city of Nassau and seizes supplies for the Continental Army.

March 4–5

Patriots seize Dorchester Heights overlooking Boston. It convinces British General William Howe that Boston is lost to the British.

March 17

Patriot troops force the British to begin evacuating Boston. The British sail for Halifax, Nova Scotia, in Canada.

April

The Hessians prepare to leave for North America. King George encourages British and Irish men to enlist in the British Royal Navy.

April 3

Congress allows privateers to attack British ships. Privateers, which are privately owned merchant ships outfitted for war, supplement the Continental Navy's 27 ships.

April 6

Congress allows the export of goods to any country in the world *not* under British rule.

EARLY PATRIOT GAINS

1776

May
Patriots build defenses in New York City, Boston, and Charlestown.

May 4
Rhode Island declares its freedom from England.

May 1–July 5
Patriot forces retreat from Canada.

May 10
Congress advises all colonies to form new governments.

June 1–28
The British Navy moves against Charlestown, attacking patriot troops at Fort Sullivan. Bad weather prevents the British from bombarding the fort. British ships open fire on the fort June 28. The British suffer major losses in the battle. Colonial Colonel William Moultrie leads an effective defense. The fort is renamed in his honor.

June 8
British General Henry Clinton lands troops on Long Island, N.Y.

June 7
Richard Henry Lee, Virginia patriot, asks Congress to declare total independence from Great Britain, form foreign alliances, and develop a plan to unite the colonies.

June 11

Congress appoints five of its members, called the Committee of Five, to write the Declaration of Independence: Thomas Jefferson (Va.), John Adams (Mass.), Benjamin Franklin (Pa.), Roger Sherman (Conn.), and Robert Livingston (N.Y.). Congress also appoints a second committee to develop a form of government for the independent colonies. This committee writes the Articles of Confederation.

Franklin (from left), Adams, Jefferson

June 10

Spain offers to sell supplies to the colonies.

Mid-June

Colonists open the Port of Boston two years after the British closed it.

June 29

General George Washington writes to Congress to announce that the British fleet has arrived at New York Harbor.

June 28

Jefferson presents a draft of the Declaration of Independence to Congress.

DECLARING
INDEPENDENCE

July 2

A British Army of 10,000 men lands on Staten Island, N.Y.

Congress adopts Richard Henry Lee's June 7 resolution for independence.

July 4

Congress adopts the Declaration of Independence after much editing and revising.

1776

July 6

John Hancock sends the Declaration of Independence to colonies asking them to proclaim the news to all.

July 5

Congress prints copies of the Declaration of Independence.

July 9

In New York City Continental soldiers and civilian patriots pull down a statue of King George III. The 4,000 pounds (1,814 kg) of lead in the statue are melted down to make musket balls.

July 12

British Admiral Richard Howe joins the fleet on Staten Island with 150 transport ships. The British troops land on Long Island with 32,000 soldiers, including 9,000 Hessians.

The first draft of the Articles of Confederation is presented to Congress. The Articles will become the first constitution of the U.S.

July 29

North and South Carolina militia troops invade Cherokee Indian territory on the North Carolina border to prevent the Cherokees from joining the British. By the time the raids are over, troops destroy 32 Indian towns and villages.

July 28

British and American troops arrive in Horn's Hook, N.Y., on the same day.

July/August

The Declaration of Independence reaches the colonies, where it is read aloud to cheers and gunshots.

British agents encourage Indians to attack colonists along frontiers from Virginia to Georgia.

LOSING TO SMALLPOX
AND THE BRITISH ARMY

1776

August

New Jersey requires men who refuse to join the militia to pay a fine.

SMALLPOX

Smallpox is a contagious disease caused by a virus. British soldiers had already been exposed to smallpox in Europe, so most were immune. But most colonists were not. Thousands caught the virus. Symptoms included fever, headache, vomiting, severe backache, and bubbles on the skin called pox. About 30 to 40 percent of those who got smallpox died. Smallpox first hit the Continental Army in Boston in 1775 and later struck patriot forces on their way to Canada in May 1776. At one time a report stated that 900 of 1,900 soldiers were sick with smallpox.

Aug. 22

British General Howe moves 20,000 soldiers into position near Washington's troops on Brooklyn Heights overlooking Manhattan.

Aug. 12

Washington writes that his army has lost many men to smallpox.

Aug. 2

Members of Congress sign the Declaration of Independence.

Aug. 14

Congress passes a bill to grant free land to any British soldier who deserts the British Army. (Soldiers have little chance of owning land in Great Britain.)

Aug. 27

British forces defeat patriots at the Battle of Long Island.

Congress offers free land to German soldiers willing to desert the British.

Sept. 9

The Second Continental Congress makes the term "United States" official.

Aug. 29

General Howe fails to stop Washington and his army's escape across the East River to Manhattan.

Sept. 11

A peace conference on Staten Island fails. British General Howe demands that Americans revoke the Declaration of Independence. Americans refuse.

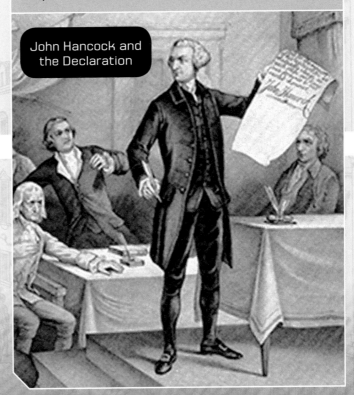

John Hancock and the Declaration

Sept. 15

British troops under General Howe occupy New York City.

BRITISH TAKE
MANHATTAN

1776

Oct. 14

Congress sends $500,000 to New York to pay a bonus to all soldiers who re-enlist. (General Washington has said that soldiers are deserting the Continental Army.)

Oct. 18

The Battle of Pell's Point delays the British advance north of New York City.

November

General Washington moves the Continental Army to New Jersey.

Sept. 21–22

The British capture and hang American spy Nathan Hale. Popular accounts claim that he declares: "My only regret is that I have but one life to lose for my country."

Sept. 22

Fire destroys much of New York City. The city has 22,000 inhabitants, making it the second biggest city after Philadelphia.

Oct. 28

The Battle of White Plains brings heavy casualties to the British.

Nov. 7

Connecticut Governor Jonathan Trumbull forbids the export of such products as salt, corn, flour, and cloth—supplies needed by the Continental Army.

Nov. 16

8,000 British troops attack and capture Fort Washington, the last American stronghold in Manhattan. The British remove American supplies and now control Manhattan Island.

Dec. 8

6,000 to 8,000 British troops land in Newport.

Dec. 12

Congress abandons Philadelphia and moves to Baltimore.

Dec. 21

Congress sends Benjamin Franklin, Arthur Lee, Thomas Jefferson, and Connecticut patriot Silas Deane to Paris to borrow money from France, longtime enemy of the British.

Dec. 6

British forces occupy the naval base at Newport, R.I.

Dec. 10

Congress warns that British troops are approaching Philadelphia and urges all colonists to unite and resist the British. Washington and his troops reach Pennsylvania the next day.

Dec. 25–26

Washington crosses the Delaware River for a surprise attack on Hessian troops at Trenton, N.J., early on Dec. 26. The Continental Army captures nearly 1,000 Hessians and their supplies while losing only five men.

WINS AND LOSSES
ON BOTH SIDES

Jan. 2

British General Charles Cornwallis and 6,000 British soldiers march toward General Washington and the Continental Army at Trenton.

Jan. 6

Washington establishes winter quarters at Morristown, N.J.

June 13

The Marquis de Lafayette, a young Frenchman who sides with the Americans, arrives in South Carolina to aid the patriots. He serves as a volunteer without pay but is later given the rank of major general.

1777

Jan. 3

Washington attacks the British rear guard at Princeton, N.J. 40 patriots and 275 British are killed. The British are driven toward New Brunswick, N.J. Washington's win encourages Americans.

May 20

The Cherokees turn all their land over to the state of South Carolina in the Treaty of DeWitts Corner.

June 14

Congress adopts the Stars and Stripes as its national flag.

July 6

General Burgoyne captures Fort Ticonderoga on Lake Champlain, N.Y

Aug. 25

British General Howe begins a campaign to capture Philadelphia.

Sept. 9–11

British and American troops clash at Philadelphia.

Sept. 21

The British inflict heavy casualties on Americans at Paoli, Pa.

Sept. 19

Patriots withstand a British attack at the First Battle of Saratoga, N.Y.

June 17–Oct. 17

British General John Burgoyne leads an invasion from Canada into New York, designed to cut the U.S. into two parts.

July

Defeat by frontier militia units forces the Cherokee Indians to give up land in Virginia and North Carolina.

Aug. 16

Patriot forces defeat British troops near Bennington, Vt.

Sept. 11

The British defeat patriots at Brandywine Creek, Pa.

Sept. 26

British troops occupy Philadelphia.

THE TURNING
POINT OF THE WAR

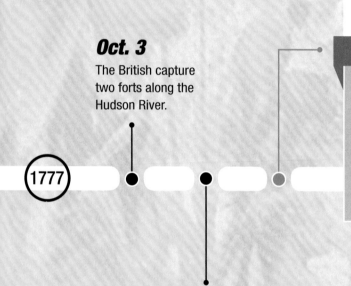

John Burgoyne

Oct. 3

The British capture two forts along the Hudson River.

Oct. 7

Patriots defeat the British at the Second Battle of Saratoga. Many experts consider this the turning point of the war. It leads General Burgoyne to surrender his army 10 days later and opens the door to aid from France.

Nov. 15

Congress adopts the Articles of Confederation and sends it to the states for ratification. It takes until March 1, 1781, for all 13 states to approve it.

1777

Oct. 4

Patriots launch a failed assault on the British at Germantown, Pa.

Oct. 17

General Burgoyne surrenders his army at Saratoga to American General Horatio Gates. About 1,400 British soldiers have been killed, captured, or wounded in the battles. The remaining 5,700 surrender their weapons. They are granted "free passage" home if they agree not to re-enter the war.

Dec. 19

George Washington's army enters winter camp at Valley Forge, Pa. Freezing weather and a lack of food, clothing, and blankets lead to illness, death, and desertion among the troops.

Feb. 6

Congress signs a treaty of alliance with France. The French help Americans develop trade with other nations and buy supplies needed to win the war.

April 22

Congress replies that the U.S. will not negotiate with Great Britain unless the British withdraw their ships and armies and recognize the U.S. as an independent nation. The British refuse.

1778

March 16

The British establish the Peace Commission of 1778 in a final attempt to make peace. They had been shocked by the defeat at Saratoga and offer the colonies self-rule.

April 22–23

John Paul Jones, a captain in the Continental Navy, leads a naval raid on Whitehaven, England. It is the only battle of the Revolution to take place in Great Britain.

NO CLEAR WINNERS

May 1

American forces try to block British supply lines into Philadelphia. The British launch a surprise attack on them. American General John Lacey leads his troops out of danger, losing only nine men. The British lose 36 men.

May 15

Patriot George Rogers Clark leads the Kentucky militia in a campaign to control British lands in what later becomes Missouri and Illinois.

AMERICAN INDIANS AND THE REVOLUTION

Many of the various native tribes living in North America chose to stay out of the conflict. But some, particularly in the northeast, joined the patriots. Others had a long history of British support. The Cherokee, for example, went to war early. They felt that colonists were moving into their territory, and the Cherokee expected the British to protect Indian lands. For years colonists and Indians battled over land. American Indians were not fighting for the British, but for their own survival.

June 19

George Washington's army leaves Valley Forge.

Henry Clinton

May 8

General Henry Clinton replaces General Howe in command of British forces in North America.

May 30

The British encourage loyalists and Indians to terrorize American settlements along the western borders of New York, Pennsylvania, and Georgia.

June 17

Word is received that France officially enters the war against Great Britain.

June 18

British forces abandon Philadelphia and cross into northeastern New Jersey after learning that France has entered the war.

1778

July 2

The Continental Congress returns to Philadelphia.

July 3

About 900 British loyalists and American Indians raid Wyoming Valley, Pa., killing more than 200 colonial militiamen.

Dec 29

A British force of about 3,500 men takes Savannah, Ga., by sea.

Nov. 11

Loyalists and Indians attack Cherry Valley, N.Y. 40 settlers die and 70 are taken prisoner.

June 28

The Battle of Monmouth, N.J., ends with no clear winner. This is the last important battle in the North.

July 8

Washington establishes headquarters at West Point, N.Y.

Aug. 8

A combined French and American force attacks Newport but fails to force out the British.

29

PATRIOTS GAIN NORTH;
BRITISH MOVE SOUTH

Jan. 6–9

British and American troops skirmish at Fort Morris in Sunbury, Ga. The fort surrenders to the British.

April

Patriot Colonel Evan Shelby leads Tennessee riflemen in the destruction of Chickamauga settlements—a successful attempt to stop Indian raids.

May–September

Washington orders troops to destroy Indian lands in upstate New York to stop raids. The Iroquois never fully recover.

May 10

American General Benedict Arnold begins providing the British with information, becoming a traitor.

1779

Jan. 31

A combined force of loyalists and British troops takes control of Augusta, Ga.

Andrew Pickens

Feb. 14

At the Battle of Kettle Creek, Colonel Andrew Pickens leads the South Carolina militia to defeat loyalists led by Colonel James Boyd. Northern Georgia is in patriot control, but southern Georgia remains under British rule.

Early May

The British raid and burn Portsmouth and Norfolk, Va.

June 21

Spain declares war on Great Britain.

July 5–11

British ships raid the Connecticut coast, burning homes and ships.

July 24–Aug. 13

The British destroy the entire Massachusetts Navy on the Penobscot River in Maine.

Aug. 14

Congress issues a peace plan that calls for American independence and British evacuation.

Aug. 29

Americans defeat a loyalist and Indian force near Elmira, N.Y.

Sept. 3–Oct. 28

American General Benjamin Lincoln and a Polish cavalry officer, Count Casimir Pulaski, lay siege to Savannah in an effort to recapture it. Pulaski, who supported the American fight for independence, dies in the battle. French and American troops suffer heavy losses.

July 16

American General Anthony Wayne leads a surprise attack on the British fort at Stony Point, N.Y., and takes it from the British.

Aug. 19

The British are forced out of New Jersey.

Sept. 1–15

American General John Sullivan destroys 40 Seneca and Cayuga villages in response to their acts of terror against American settlers.

Oct. 17

The Continental Army establishes winter quarters at Morristown, N.J. Conditions are worse than at Valley Forge. Many soldiers desert and protests increase.

PATRIOTS SUFFER
STINGING LOSSES

January

Patriots stage surprise attacks on British troops, especially in Georgia and South Carolina. Patriots often attack from woods and swamps, hide behind trees, and swoop down on the British without warning.

Feb. 1

British General Clinton arrives off the coast of South Carolina with a fleet carrying 8,000 soldiers.

May 7

Fort Moultrie on Sullivan Island off Charlestown falls to the British.

May 12

In the worst American defeat of the Revolution, General Benjamin Lincoln surrenders the city of Charlestown, about 5,000 troops, several naval vessels, and nearly 400 pieces of artillery to the British.

1780

Jan. 1

100 Massachusetts soldiers mutiny at West Point. They want to return home when their enlistments are up.

April 8

The British begin an attack on Charlestown.

May 29

A Virginia regiment, the only remaining patriot force in South Carolina, is destroyed by British Colonel Banastre Tarleton and his British raiders at Waxhaw Creek, S.C.

July 25

General Horatio Gates takes command of patriot forces in the South.

Aug. 18

In the Battle of Fishing Creek, S.C., British Colonel Tarleton surprises the Americans, killing 150 and taking 300 prisoner.

Oct. 7

American militias defeat loyalists at Kings Mountain, S.C.

May 25

Connecticut regiments mutiny at Washington's camp at Morristown.

July 12

Patriots launch a surprise attack against loyalist Captain Christian Huck at Williamson's Plantation, S.C., killing Huck and up to 50 of his men.

Aug. 16

Patriots suffer heavy losses to the British at Camden, S.C., with as many as 900 Americans killed and up to 1,000 captured.

Sept. 29

American militia leader Francis Marion, known as the Swamp Fox, leads patriots on a surprise attack against loyalists at Black Mingo Creek, S.C.

TIRED
OF WAR

Jan. 1–10

Pennsylvania soldiers mutiny. Soldiers want food, supplies, and more pay. Many are eager to go home to families and farms.

Jan. 17

Americans defeat Tarleton's British troops at the Battle of Cowpens, S.C. British losses include nearly 1,000 casualties. The win raises patriot confidence.

March 18

British forces march to Wilmington, N.C., to await reinforcements.

April 2

Two British ships, *Mars* and *Minerva*, attack the American frigate *Alliance*. Patriot commander John Barry forces the British to surrender.

Jan. 5

British troops led by Benedict Arnold burn Richmond, Va.

Jan. 20–27

New Jersey troops mutiny. Two leaders are executed on the spot to discourage further mutiny.

March 1–2

Maryland becomes the final state to ratify the Articles of Confederation. The Articles guide the nation until the Constitution is ratified in 1788.

March 15

The British win the Battle at Guilford Courthouse, N.C., but suffer heavy losses in the process.

May 15

The Continental Army takes Fort Granby, S.C., from the British. Patriots gain an important position, ammunition, and supplies without losing any men.

May 26

Congress, meeting in Philadelphia, approves a national bank.

June 4

British General Cornwallis plans to capture Virginia Governor Thomas Jefferson and the Virginia Legislature. Jefferson is warned in time and all patriots escape uninjured. Jefferson, elected in 1779, is the state's second governor. Patrick Henry was the first.

May 22–June 18

Americans retreat after failing to take Ninety Six, S.C., an important and heavily fortified town. The 550 loyalists defending the town kill or wound 185 patriots.

June 10

Benedict Arnold leads British raiding parties near Richmond.

June 19

American forces stop British raids in Virginia.

June 5

Americans recapture Augusta.

July 6

At the Battle of Green Spring, Va., a force of 900 Americans fights 7,000 British soldiers. When they realize the size of the British forces, the Americans retreat. Patriot losses tally 28 dead, 99 wounded, and 12 missing.

Aug. 30

A French fleet arrives at Yorktown with 3,000 troops.

Sept. 6

Benedict Arnold leads British troops to burn New London, Conn.

Sept. 8

American General Nathanael Greene leads a fight at Eutaw Springs, S.C. There is no clear winner, but Americans push the British back to Charlestown. Most of South Carolina is now under American control.

1781

Aug. 1

British General Cornwallis establishes a base at Yorktown.

Sept. 5–9

24 French warships defeat a British fleet of 19 warships at the entrance to Chesapeake Bay. The British retreat. French forces take control, trapping the British Army on the Yorktown Peninsula.

Sept. 14–25

American and French troops reach Williamsburg, Va.

Sept. 28

American and French troops begin a siege of the British at Yorktown. Combined forces of nearly 17,000 American and French troops surround British General Cornwallis and his 9,000 men. Americans begin round-the-clock artillery bombardment of the British.

Oct. 24

Congress learns of the victory at Yorktown and goes to a nearby church to give thanks.

Sept. 30

The British abandon outer defenses at Yorktown.

Nov. 7

300 loyalists fire on 30 patriots at Cloud's Creek, S.C. Only 2 patriots survive.

Dec. 28–29

British troops are posted at Charlestown after they leave Wilmington.

Oct. 19

Cornwallis surrenders at Yorktown.

Nov.18

British troops evacuate Wilmington.

GOOD-BYE LOYALISTS

Jan. 1
Loyalists begin to leave. Some return to England. Others go to Canada, Spanish-controlled Florida, or British-owned islands in the Caribbean.

April 12
Peace talks begin in Paris. American delegates John Jay, John Adams, and Benjamin Franklin attend.

July 11
The British evacuate Savannah.

August
Loyalists and American Indians conduct raids into settlements along the Pennsylvania, Ohio, Virginia, and Kentucky frontier. News has not reached them that Cornwallis surrendered.

1782

Jan. 5
The British Army leaves Wilmington and begins withdrawing from other occupied ports and cities.

June 20
Congress adopts the Great Seal of the U.S.

Aug. 7

George Washington creates the Purple Heart, an award to recognize soldiers wounded in battle. The medal is still given today.

September

Jay, Adams, and Franklin begin direct negotiations with the British.

Nov. 30

In Paris, Franklin, Jay, and Adams negotiate a peace treaty with the British.

Nov. 10

George Rogers Clark and a large force retaliate against the British for the August attacks on the frontier.

Dec. 14

British troops leave Charlestown.

Dec. 24

French troops leave Boston.

Aug. 27

British and American troops skirmish in South Carolina. It is the last action in the eastern U.S.

PEACE
AT LAST

1783

Feb. 3
Spain recognizes the U.S. as an independent nation.

Feb. 4
King George III of Great Britain officially declares an end to the war.

April 11
U.S. Congress proclaims an official end to hostilities.

April 15
U.S. Congress approves a version of the peace treaty.

May 30
The U.S.'s first daily newspaper, the *Pennsylvania Evening Post*, begins publication in Philadelphia.

June
Soldiers demand back pay and march on Philadelphia. Members of Congress flee to Princeton, N.J. They have no money, so they turn the problem over to the states.

July 8
Massachusetts Supreme Court abolishes slavery in the state.

SLAVERY AND THE REVOLUTION

There were 450,000 African slaves in the 13 colonies in 1775. Every colony allowed slavery. During the war the British offered freedom to slaves who fought for them. Fewer than 1,000 did so. About 5,000 African-Americans fought on the patriot side. White and black soldiers often fought side by side. This helped to end slavery in New England at the end of the war. Between 1780 and 1804, New York, Pennsylvania, and New Jersey gradually freed slaves. Discrimination did not end, however, and slavery remained strong in southern states.

Sept. 3

The U.S. and Great Britain sign the Treaty of Paris. The treaty establishes national borders, defines fishing rights, and returns property to loyalists. It also allows the use of the Mississippi River by both Americans and British, and it makes evacuation of British forces possible. The treaty allows money to be transferred between Great Britain and the U.S.

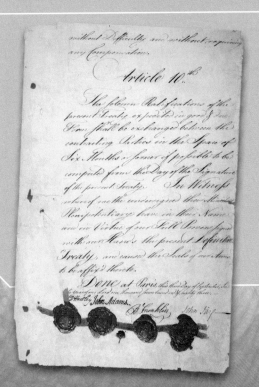

November

The Continental Army disbands. The U.S. Army replaces it.

Dec. 23

George Washington resigns as commander of the Continental Army and retires to Virginia.

Oct. 7

Virginia frees all slaves who fought for independence during the war.

Nov. 25

The British Army leaves New York City—its last military position in the U.S.—and Washington enters.

Thomas Jefferson Memorial

Jan. 14

Congress ratifies the Treaty of Paris. It establishes the boundaries of the U.S. and recommends that loyalists be treated fairly.

1784

1786

Jan. 16

Virginia adopts the Statute for Religious Freedom, written by Thomas Jefferson. It states that no Virginian will face prosecution because of religious beliefs. The statute becomes a model for the idea of religious freedom later included in the U.S. Bill of Rights.

May 7

John Jay is named U.S. secretary for foreign affairs.

Feb. 20

New Jersey challenges Congress over fees. Congress had charged each state $3 million to support the federal government and pay foreign debts. Ten of the 13 states agreed to the payments, but few have paid.

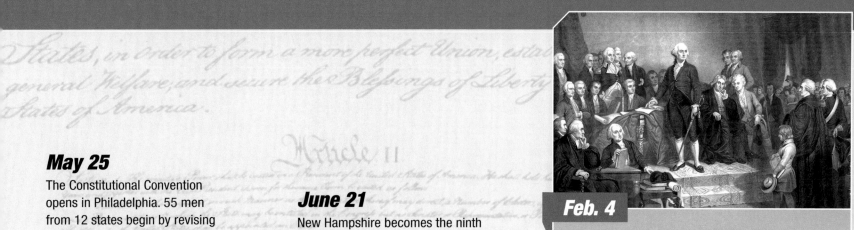

May 25

The Constitutional Convention opens in Philadelphia. 55 men from 12 states begin by revising the Articles of Confederation.

June 21

New Hampshire becomes the ninth state to ratify the Constitution.

Feb. 4

George Washington is elected the first president of the United States and serves until 1797.

1787

1788

1789

Sept. 17

The final draft of the U.S. Constitution is read to 42 delegates. 39 sign the document and tell Congress that their work is complete. Nine states will be needed to ratify the document.

July 2

Congress declares the Constitution to be in effect and issues instructions for choosing representatives to Congress and electing the first president.

THE COSTS AND REWARDS
OF INDEPENDENCE

Guided by the Constitution and under the leadership of President George Washington, Congress established a new government. State representatives argued over the form of government, expenses, and the nation's future, but they all agreed on one thing—they must work to preserve their hard-won independence. Congress established relationships with foreign countries and gradually built a nation from colonies that had been hammered by war.

During the long war, battles took place in every state except New Hampshire. The western frontier—the border areas of western New York, Pennsylvania, Virginia, the Carolinas, and Georgia—had suffered frequent skirmishes between patriot militias and groups of loyalists and American Indians. The British had captured almost every major American city at some point during the eight-year war.

Despite the difficulties, the patriots never gave up. More than 200,000 Americans fought in the war. More than 7,400 died in battle, and about 8,000 died in British prisons. Another 10,000 died from disease or illness. While men fought the actual battles, women and children helped in other ways. They maintained homes, farms, and businesses. Some became spies or followed the Army to cook, clean, and care for the wounded.

Great Britain did not escape the costs of war either. Thousands of British soldiers died. More than 60,000 loyalists fled their homes in the United States at the end of the war. The financial cost of war increased Britain's debt. Trade was interrupted and thousands of British merchant ships were captured.

The war brought about many other changes in the new country. South Carolina and Georgia lost one-fourth to one-third of their slaves. Several northern states took a serious look at the problems caused by slavery. Many states outlawed it. Others moved more slowly toward freeing their enslaved people. For American Indians, the Revolution signaled devastating changes. As the new nation grew, settlers claimed more and more Indian hunting grounds.

What began as a small collection of colonies gradually grew to be a major world power. From 13 colonies to 50 states, the United States built upon the strengths and beliefs its founders demonstrated. The country continues to grow and still strives to ensure "life, liberty, and the pursuit of happiness" for its citizens. It all began with the American Revolution.

GLOSSARY

alliance—an agreement between nations or groups of people to work together

boycott—to refuse to buy or use a product or service to protest something believed to be wrong or unfair

casualty—a person killed, wounded, or missing in a battle or in a war

congress—an official meeting of representatives from various nations, states, or colonies

delegate—a person who represents a larger group of people at a meeting

frigate—a warship used in the 1700s and 1800s

legislature—a group of elected officials who have the power to make or change laws for a country or state

loyalist—a colonist who was loyal to Great Britain during the Revolutionary War

militia—a group of volunteer citizens who are organized to fight, but who are not professional soldiers

musket—a gun with a long barrel that was used before the rifle was invented

mutiny—a rebellion of soldiers against their officers

occupy—to take possession or control by military invasion

Parliament—the national legislature of Great Britain

patriot—a person who sided with the colonies during the Revolutionary War

ratify—to formally approve

resolution—a formal expression of opinion, will, or intent voted on by an official body or assembled group

revolution—an uprising by a group of people against a system of government or a way of life

treaty—a formal agreement between groups or nations

READ MORE

Catel, Patrick. *Key People of the Revolutionary War.*
Chicago: Heinemann Library, 2011.

Forest, Christopher. *The Biggest Battles of the Revolutionary War.*
North Mankato, Minn.: Capstone Press, 2013.

Murphy, Jim. *The Crossing: How George Washington Saved the
American Revolution.* New York: Scholastic, 2010.

Raum, Elizabeth. *True Stories of the Revolutionary War.*
North Mankato, Minn.: Capstone Press, 2013.

INTERNET SITES

Use FactHound to find Internet sites related to this book.
All of the sites on FactHound have been researched by our staff.

Here's all you do:

Visit www.facthound.com

Type in this code: 9781476541570

INDEX